TAILOR-MADE SUCCESS FOR ENTREPRENUERS

FROM A LIFETIME OF EXPERIENCES BY ART LEWIN

Published By Wadsworth Publishing

ACKNOWLEDGMENTS

"In my walks, every man I meet is my superior in some way, and in that I learn from him."

— Ralph Waldo Emerson

A million thanks ...

To my mother for teaching me perseverance and telling me that I can do it! Te Amo, Mami.

To my father for teaching me discipline and telling me to be the best at whatever I do. He always said, "do it right or don't do it at all." Gracias, Papi.

To my grandmother Irma for her unconditional love.

To my kids, Alexis, Amanda, and little Art, for always being there for me, especially since we have been through times when I couldn't be there for you. I love you so much.

To my mentors, Victor Vaswani, Craig Tshudi, Ray Montalvo, Judge Patricia Schwartz, Michael Papale, Jack Taylor, and many others for the eye-opening education.

To my friends and family who have been a part of my life's journey and have put up with my ramblings about life, relationships, salesmanship, business, and other things. Christian Lewin, Max Lewin, Hans Lewin, Lisbett Lewin, Michael & Nicole Papale, Alex Diaz, Anthony & Lisa Navarro, Hector & Yatzel Rendon, Doug Carlton, Scott and David Cacurak, Richard Taylor, Edwin Tuazon, Armen and Marine Makaryan, Jerry Bakhchyan, Barry Fischer, Tia Sylvia, Tia Eli, Tio Carlos, Ericka & Alisha Lewin, Donnie & Melissa Gasaway, Ben and Nichole Hoss, Sarah Bakhtiar, Ricardo & Vicky

Abrines, Edgar Padilla & family, Craig & Mandy Thomas, Rande & Rosemary Ferguson, and many who I haven't named here, you are all amazing.

To my clients for their loyalty and confidence in my company, my product, and me. Without you, I wouldn't have been able to write my life story.

To Team Lewin for doing the amazing work they do from scheduling appointments to tailoring and assisting, as well as for enabling me to dress thousands of clients every year.

And to my beautiful wife, Jamie, for always sharing your food even when you don't want to, for doing all that needs to be done to make our life and business better, for listening to all my dreams and ambitions, and for having faith in me that I will achieve all my dreams and ambitions. Thank you for being my confidant, my cheerleader, my best friend, my lover, and my wife. You make my life beautiful.

Thank you all for being a part of this gift of my adventurous life.

Table of Contents

ACKNOWLEDGMENTS II

CHAPTER 1 – MY LIFETIME INGREDIENTS FOR SUCCESS IN BUSINESS, SELLING, AND LIFE 1

CHAPTER 2 – I DID NOT GET THIS FAR BY LUCK 17

CHAPTER 3 – ART'S SEARCH WHY SOME SUCCEED AND OTHERS FAIL IN SALES AND BUSINESS 31

CHAPTER 4 – TEN COMMON HABITS OF SUCCESSFUL PEOPLE 42

CHAPTER 5 – NETWORKING 56

CHAPTER 6 – LESSONS LEARNED FROM MY EXTREMELY SUCCESSFUL AND POWERFUL CLIENTS 71

CHAPTER 7 – TWELVE WAYS TO GET MORE BUSINESS 89

CHAPTER 8 – MY THOUGHTS 119

ABOUT THE AUTHOR 130

Chapter 1 – My Lifetime Ingredients for Success in

Business, Selling, and Life

My story is about passion, obsession, purpose, drive, and discipline. You might call me a writer since you are reading a book I wrote, but I am not a writer. In fact, English is my second language.

After knowing this, you might want to call me lucky, but I would disagree. Here is why ...

My story began in Vina del Mar, Chile. I was born on March 21st, 1967. My father came to the United States in 1970, and my mother followed two years later. So, I do not remember seeing my parents much during the years I spent in Chile.

My parents had moved to the United States in hopes of finding a better future for my four siblings and me while we lived with our grandparents. Life was difficult in Chile, if not dangerous. There were food shortages and unregulated inflation under President Salvador Allende. When General Augusto Pinochet took over the government in 1973, there began a series of disappearances and assassinations, of which a few I witnessed and even remember to this day. Other than that, I do not remember much about my life in Chile besides going to school, playing in the park, and playing near our local church.

On the other hand, I vividly remember my journey to the United States. Whenever I tell someone about that journey, I mention the movie *Planes, Trains, and Automobiles,* as that was how the journey was for my family and me.

Years later, my father came to Chile one day and took my second brother Christian and me with him back to the US. He could not afford to take all the kids, so my other two brothers and my sister could not join us. We took a plane, and then some trains, and automobiles, as well as a boat through south and central America.

Though the trip was long, I do not remember being too tired or scared. There were definitely some tense moments, of course, as the hostel in San Salvador had many spider webs all along its corridors. We had to walk through the corridor many times since the bathroom was down the hall. I found out only after growing up that those spiders I thought were so frightening were the least dangerous thing about that hostel.

When we arrived in Mexico, we got caught by agents from Mexico's border control department. My father mislead them by saying that we were from Guatemala. That way, they do not send all the way back to Chile. We were sent over to the Mexican-Guatemalan border, from where we crossed the border again into Mexico only a short while later.

It took us almost a month from the time we had left Chile to get to the Mexico-US border, crossing, which was like a military operation. There was a river that I crossed on my elbows, along with other men, women, and other children.

We also ran across Interstate 5 in Southern California, resembling the image of the immigrant family on the yellow caution sign on the highway near San Diego. I also remember telling my father that the highway was the largest street I had ever seen. At that time, we didn't have freeways in Chile.

When we finally made it to the safety of a car, my brother and I were stowed in the trunk. It seemed an eternity. On our way to Los Angeles later, we were transferred to a van. It was then that I saw the Spanish-language names of the cities we were passing through, namely San Diego, Chula Vista, Del Mar, La Jolla, Escondido, Santa Ana, Los Angeles, etc., and got confused if we had arrived in the United States or not.

It finally struck me that we were in the United States when we arrived at our studio apartment in Van Nuys, and we were exposed to the strange custom of kids in costumes knocking on our door asking *"tricks or treat?"* I was eight years old at the time, and my brother Christian was seven. It took my father several years to be able to go back to Chile and bring back my remaining siblings. They took the same journey as Christian and I took with our father. It was a total of eight or nine years before all of us would be reunited in the United States.

Settling down and fitting into a completely different society was a problem that was bigger than it first seemed to be. But I remember a quote by Norman Vincent Peale whenever I'm faced with a problem. It goes like:

"The only people I have ever known to have no problems are those in the cemetery."

There were few, if any, ESL classes in public schools back in the 70s. I knew only a few English words when I had arrived in the United States, but I learned it quickly. In fact, I was forced to learn it quickly. The first friend I made when I got to this country taught me English between periods. It was one of the few positive aspects of my early educational experiences in the US. I was bussed to different schools all the time; otherwise. One year, I would be going to a middle school in Hollywood, and a couple of years later, I was bussed to a school in south-central Los Angeles. I did not learn much in that environment except how to get into trouble.

It was not just the changing schools I had to adjust to. I also had to adjust to the reality of not having my father around. Following their divorce, my father had left my mother and had left her alone in raising their five kids.

My mother supported us by cleaning houses and later was contracted to clean several gas station bathrooms. By the time I turned 12, I was already driving and helping my mother clean bathrooms, as well as taking up other jobs to support the family. When my friends asked me why I did not join them after school. I would lie to them and tell them that I was taking my mother to class to learn English.

Looking back, in some ways, I am grateful for the experiences I had with my mother. The work we had to do to survive and my transformation into the act of a father-like of the family meant that I had to learn how to hustle incredibly early in life. My hunger and my drive were born in the summer nights when we would all wake up in a pool of sweat, living in our 900 square foot house in Van Nuys in the San Fernando Valley with no air conditioning and one bathroom. My desire for a better life was reinforced with every bathroom I helped my mother clean, and with every moment, I watched her try her best to help the family survive. I cannot begin to tell you how disgusting those gas station bathrooms were. They inculcated in me the quality of hustling. It became a part of me from my earliest years in this country.

There is a difference between hustling to survive and hustling to thrive, and it took me some time to learn the difference. During my junior high and high school years, I had many friends that were in the streets selling drugs, involved in theft, or other activities that eventually led to jail or some other dead end. I readily confess that this was almost my path as well, until a judge woke me up in my early 20s, making me realize that I could be facing substantial jail time for the crimes I was committing.

There were some other people in my circle that provided examples of a life to which I aspired. I had a health teacher who dressed well, drove a fancy car, and taught me a skill that I use to this day: visualizing a path to success. I also had an uncle in Chicago who was a senior executive at the Tribune Company, which made me think that if he could be successful, I could be successful too. My father got us into cycling to keep us out of trouble and teaching us about hard work, determination & self-discipline. I still use those principles today. I also experienced first-hand the lifestyle that success could bring through a girlfriend I had in high school. We would go to fancy restaurants with her parents as they drove us in their Mercedes Benz, and I would tell myself that I would live like this one day.

While I vividly remember my journey to the United States, the fact that I was undocumented was less central in my life than the everyday struggle to help my family survive. My mother had begun working on the legalization process for the family not long after my parents divorced. I was in high school when I finally received a social security number, which is when I realized my legal status had shifted. Nevertheless, I readily admit that I came to this country undocumented. Why shouldn't I? This is part of my life's story, and it makes me so proud to think of where I came from and what I have been able to provide for my family.

Though I had to learn how to hustle early in life, my path towards the custom clothing business I have today started when I began working in sales. I was 18 when I started selling vacuum cleaners door to door. It was the toughest sales job I have ever had, but it did teach me the importance of accepting and learning from failure. To this day, I emphasize that failure is an important part of our training program at Art Lewin Bespoke. Shortly after I began another sales job, I was recruited by a company called Metagram America – a fortune 500 company with 3000 salesmen selling alphanumeric pagers, which in those days before cell phones allowed people to contact each other by leaving a phone number and an alphanumeric message, much like texting today. Almost immediately, I became the TOP salesman in the company and became a branch sales manager at a young age, leading veterans' in the pager business.

It was in 1989, the year that my life changed for the best. It was that one day I sold two alphanumeric pagers to a custom clothier. He was impressed with my sales experience & ability and recruited me into the clothing business. I worked with Victor for several years, then I went off to work for the largest custom clothing companies in the world, learning about the clothing business from every angle that I could learn, before starting my own custom clothing business in 1997.

Being an entrepreneur is rarely an easy or smooth road. Growing my own business meant building a client base from scratch. This meant I spent long hours during the first few years of my business, rarely seeing my first wife and kids. However, my determination and attention to understanding the needs of my clients (such as making the fitting process as convenient as possible by going to their place of business) allowed me to scale my business to more than 2,000 clients within a couple of years.

The key challenges of building and maintaining a business are learning from failure and finding the strength to move forward even in the most catastrophic of circumstances. I sell a luxury product, after all, which makes my business inherently vulnerable to the ups and downs of the economy. In 2008, the business I had worked so hard to build began to collapse as a result of the economic downturn, combined with a huge audit from the IRS. Around this time, my strong, beautiful mother, the woman who had worked so hard to provide for my family and me, was diagnosed with cancer with only a five percent chance of survival. I was fighting for my mother's life and for the survival of my business at the same time, though I would have willingly given up everything I had to ensure my mother's survival. Thankfully, my mother did survive, and I celebrate her every time I see her.

Meanwhile, this downturn allowed me to renovate my business and pick up a whole new clientele just by changing one word in the name of my business. I changed the name of my business from Art Lewin Clothiers to Art Lewin Bespoke. Back then, typically, the super-wealthy knew about the word bespoke; it is more of an English term meaning bespoke for you. Our suits are made just for you and not off a pattern.

In 2009, I came back stronger with a new and larger clientele base. This period also helped me reflect on how I could start giving back to the local community, speaking to local youth, and making philanthropic donations to several organizations.

Occasionally, I had had the chance to drive the freeway that I crossed with my family when we first arrived in this country. Sometimes, I go back and visit the 900 square foot house that I grew up in with my siblings. I think about these periods in my life, and sometimes I begin to cry out of gratitude for what I have been able to accomplish.

I know that my life has turned out quite differently compared to many of my friends from junior high and high school and compared to some members of my own family. I think the fact that I had little choice but to hustle at an early age helped me to develop what I call a Ph.D. mentality – staying **positive, hungry, and driven**. My Ph.D. was earned not in the hallowed halls of academia but in the streets of Van Nuys. My Ph.D. is honed with every success and every failure.

Chapter 2 – I Did Not Get This Far by Luck

I am just an average person with an above-average desire. I did not get this far by luck. Nobody successful I know got far by luck. Luck plays a small, if any, role in anyone's success.

Success comes from two things: hard work and discipline.

While hard work is something a lot of people know of and put in towards their goals, not many live with discipline. Therefore, I want to begin with the importance of discipline and how you can inculcate it within yourself.

Discipline is important because it gives birth to routine. When a person follows a routine, they begin to work in routine too. Some people even argue that working in routine or working consistently is even more important than working hard. When a person lives with discipline, they work with discipline too, which can lead them to work effectively and efficiently.

To be disciplined is to create a lifestyle for yourself that ensures success.

So, how can you learn to be disciplined?

Let me share five things that my successful friends and I do before 8 am in the morning.

1. RISE AND SHINE

If you want to be successful, mornings should be your best friend.

Now, you may not be a morning person. There is also the chance that you absolutely hate mornings. But, utilizing the morning hours has been called the key to a successful and healthy lifestyle.

Yes, early rising is a common trait among many of my friends who are CEOs, Government officials, or occupy other influential positions.

Did you know that Former British Prime Minister Margaret Thatcher was up every day at 5 in the morning? Also, Frank Lloyd Wright would get up at 4 am, and the CEO of Walt Disney, Robert Iger, wakes up at 4:30 am.

You must be thinking: ***but I do my best work late at night.***

Not so fast!

According to Inc. Magazine, those who work early in the morning are not only more productive and proactive than those who work at night but are also healthier.

Now, getting healthy may not be a concern to you as you think about your business. However, it should be. Let me elaborate on this in the next point.

2. EXERCISE

I have said it once, and I will say it again: most successful people work out, and they work out in the morning.

You can do whatever suits you best: a morning jog, yoga, or a trip to the gym. But do get moving once you wake up. Exercising before getting started with one's day gives one a boost of energy and the feeling of accomplishment and starting the day right. When you know you did 200 ab reps in the morning, you can easily tackle the paperwork too!

Another reason that makes working out in the mornings great is that it eliminates the possibility of flaking out on your workout later in the day, which we all know happens more often than we would like to admit.

If you're no bright-eyed and bushy about waking up at five in the morning, then begin with waking 15 minutes earlier than your usual time. Do a quick set of pushups beside the bed or do basic yoga stretches. It will help you wake up your body and will prepare you for the day.

Remember, a sound mind can only exist in a sound body, and both of these sound resources of yours will eventually help you with your business.

3. MAP OUT YOUR DAY

The day can be a bit haphazard if not planned. Take control of your day and maximize your potential by mapping out your schedule for the day. You may already have a to-do list for the day; you can take it a step further by planning the day's tasks according to their priority.

The best time to make your to-do list better is, again, the mornings. You wake up with a clear head, so it's also easier for you to make decisions and prioritize the tasks.

The early hours of the day also provide peace and quiet, and so make it a good time for some self-reflection and uninterrupted problem-solving. However, when planning the day, don't neglect your mental health. It is easy to get carried away when one feels motivated.

Therefore, as you plan your day, try to be realistic while also being productive. Don't burden yourself too much. Take into account the fact that you will get tired throughout the day. Give yourself some breaks to recover from the exhaustion of being productive.

You can schedule ten-minute breaks for yourself between tasks. In these breaks, you can go for a walk or take a moment to meditate. In the evening, take a break to plan a healthy dinner or to pack some healthy snacks for the next day.

4. EAT A HEALTHY BREAKFAST

As much as you don't want to waste time eating or believe that gulping down coffee on an empty stomach will make you productive, it won't.

It does no good. It only makes you wonder when the taco truck comes in as you sit on your desk.

Take some time in the morning to fuel your body for the day. It will keep your mind focused on the work in front of you and will not distract it by the growling of your stomach.

If you don't live alone, having breakfast can become more from only a healthy activity to a social activity. It will provide you with a good setting to bond with the people you live with, be it your spouse, kids, or a friend.

Besides, making a bowl of oatmeal or granola only takes five minutes, but keep your spirits high for hours.

5. VISUALIZATION

When you're doing all of these for your body, don't ignore your mind. It is very easy to overlook mental health when we have a lot going on in our daily lives.

It is why spending some quiet time in the mornings is great. They provide the perfect opportunity to get inside your mind, meditate, and visualize.

Take this time to visualize your day ahead. Focus on the goals you want to achieve or make progress with. A minute a day of positive thinking can go a long way by helping you improve your mood and outlook on life. Again, be realistic about the amount of work you can do and the progress you can make with your goals.

Don't try to visualize miracles. Stay on the ground and in reality. Visualization is about positive thinking, not fairytale thinking.

BONUS TIP: Start Your Day Heavy

We all have that one thing on our to-do list that we dread. It looms over us all day until, after much procrastination, we gather enough energy to suck it up and do it.

Here's an easy tip to save yourself from all that stress: do the least desirable task on your to-do list first. Reduce the time of anticipating the unpleasantness of it. Get it done between breakfast and lunch and get it out of the way.

The more you delay it, the more you will dread it. Not to mention, but your energy level will reduce throughout the day too. So it's best to do it first thing in the day. You're fresh, and you're better equipped to handle the difficult task.

Look at it this way, if you do the most difficult thing first, the rest of the day will get progressively easier, not the other way around. By the time your workday will be coming to an end, you will only be left with easy tasks. You will also head into your free time more relaxed.

SUCCESS!

I decided to write this book because I wanted people to think about their dreams. If you're reading this book, then I'm sure you're one of those dreamers, just like me.

I don't believe in death is the greatest tragedy of life. I believe it to be living one's life bound by the experiences of the past.

We all have the power to change our lives. We all have the power to achieve success, and I have learned that success comes only after you have paid its price. I have also learned that success leaves clues and that successful people map these out.

Mark Twain said, and I quote:

"The secret of getting ahead is getting started."

There is always time for each one of us to take control of our lives. Don't be scared to do it.

If you don't like where you came from, if you have done someone wrong, if you come from a broken family, if you were born poor or if you were born rich and never learned to make money if you made money but got bankrupted, if you have been abandoned or if you have suffered abuse;

remember that every person on this earth has been in at least one of these situations.

We have all been there, but it doesn't mean that we stay there. Now, the choice is yours.

Do you choose to dwell in the past?

Do you let the opinion of others become your reality?

Do you let others control your destiny?

I choose not to dwell on my past. I didn't let other's opinions stop me, and I refused to let them control my destiny.

My own struggle, my own story showed me that when one is focused and driven, and learns from the experiences and opportunities that life presents them, then anything is possible. I know I haven't made the best choices in my life or chosen the easiest paths, but I know I made a choice to persevere.

I stayed persistent, and I stayed consistent. I hope that my story can bring you hope and can help you understand what it is that you need to do to change your life.What I had to do was…

"OUTsmart, OUTsell, OUTperform, OUTdress your competition."

- Art Lewin

Chapter 3 – Art's Search Why Some Succeed and Others Fail in Sales and Business

Have you ever wondered why some succeed while others fail in business?

Don't tell me it's luck since we have already established that's not something we count on. I never believed in luck anyway, so when this question first popped in my head, I set out to do some research. I had already realized years ago that I was trying to lead and direct the efforts of a group of people towards success while not knowing the path to success myself. When I realized that, I also realized that it did not matter what skill or knowledge I brought to the job; all that mattered was that I should find the path and the secret to success.

I was on a mission. For a full year, I read biographies and interviewed my most successful clients. I came to the conclusion that the secret lied not only in what people did but in what made them do it.

It made sense, but it didn't bring my research to a halt. I still had to find a path that everyone who wanted to be successful could take, one that was applied by all those who have been successful in sales and business. I knew there must be a single thread that joined all the success stories. I found it, and I found it to be true, simple, and powerful.

Here it is:

The common thread to everyone's success, everyone who has ever been successful in sales &

business, is that these people have a purpose that is strong enough to cause them to decide to form the habits of doing things that poor performers don't like to do.

It is as simple as it seems — the secret to being successful lies in forming the habit of doing things that don't feel good.

No wonder only a few truly achieve success.

But why is a habit the key to success? Well, because humans are creatures of habits. It is our innate ability to form habits that let us do more than one thing at a time.

How are these people able to form habits that benefit them?

The answer is simple; they're driven by purpose.

PURPOSE!

It is only your purpose in life that determines your future, so let's talk about it.

You may have been discouraged by the thought or feeling that you were born with certain dislikes that most successful people don't tend to have. You may have also wondered about how your life would have been different had you actually enjoyed the things achievers tend to enjoy.

Let me tell you something: they don't!

I believe this is the single most encouraging statement I can ever make to sales and business professionals, but it is also the truest! Top sales and business achievers do not like making contacts, appointments, or sales presentations.

Now you must be wondering if they don't like doing these things, then why do they do it?

The answer to that is simple: they do these things that they don't like doing because doing them helps them achieve their purpose!

The difference between successful, unsuccessful people is simple. Successful salespeople are influenced by their burning desire for results, while poor performers are influenced more by their desire to methods that feel good and will take whatever results they can get by doing things they like to do.

But why is this so? Why are some (successful) salespeople able to do the things they do not like to do while some (unsuccessful) are not?

It is the presence of a purpose and the drive to achieve it that helps them. In other words, successful people have a purpose that is strong enough to cause them to decide to form the habit of doing things that do not feel good in order to accomplish the purpose they want to accomplish.

For a purpose to be strong enough to cause a man to change his habits, it must be practical.

Some time ago, I was talking to a man who believed he had a purpose, which was more important to him than his income. He deeply felt the suffering of his fellow men and wanted to reach a position where he would be able to alleviate that suffering. But when he truly analyzed his real feelings, he found and admitted too that what he really wanted was a good job dispensing charity with other people's money and being well paid for it, along with the appreciation and importance that would naturally come with such a job.

This is not a practical purpose.

However, when trying to make a practical purpose, be careful not to make it logical.

Instead, make your purpose sentimental or emotional.

Remember, needs are logical, while wants and desires are sentimental or emotional. Your needs will push you just so far enough, but once they are satisfied, they will stop pushing you. If, however, your purpose is tied to wants and desires, then your wants and desires will keep pushing you long after your needs are satisfied.

Sometimes even our best salespeople get into a slump. A slump is a sign that a salesperson has reached a point where things they do not like to do have become more important than their purpose.

I have had some salespeople tell me at this point,

"' but I have a family to support.' Isn't that enough purpose?"

I tell them: no, it's not. If it were a strong enough purpose, it would make them do the things that do not feel good.

I have observed that it's easier for a poor performer to adjust to the hardships than to become a better performer. If you do not believe me, think of all the things people are willing to do to keep from doing the things they do not like to do. All of this seems to prove that willpower alone is not strong enough to cause you to do things that do not feel good; it's the emotional strength of your purpose that is truly critical for your success.

Recently, I had the chance to talk to a young man who long ago discovered this principle of success without knowing his discovery. He had a definite purpose in life, and it was also a sentimental and emotional one: He wanted his boy to go to college without having to work his way through it, as he had done. He also wanted to avoid all the hardships for his wife and kids, which he, his sister, and his mother had seen, and to provide for them all the necessities, comfort, and luxuries that he was denied as a kid. This young man was also willing to form the habit of doing things he did not like to do to accomplish this purpose.

I didn't mean to discourage him, rather the opposite; I wanted him to encourage me, so I asked him, ***"aren't you going a little too far with this thing? There is no logical reason why your son should not be willing to work his way through college as his father did. Of course, he will have heartaches and disappointments, but if he's any good, he'll come through in the end just like you did. There's no logical reason why you should***

slave in order for your son to have things which you didn't have, or in order that your wife can enjoy comforts and luxuries that she wasn't used to before she married you."

He looked at me with rather a pitying look and said, *"Art, there's no inspiration in logic, there is no courage in logic, there's not even happiness in logic; there's only satisfaction. The only place logic has in my life is in the realization that the more I am willing to do for my wife and children, the more I will be able to do for myself."*

After this story, I don't think anyone needs to be told how to find their purpose, or how to identify it, or how to surrender to it. If it is a big purpose, you will be big in its accomplishment. If it's an unselfish purpose, you will be unselfish in accomplishing it. And if it is an honest purpose, you will be honest and honorable in its accomplishment.

Now, do not forget that while you succeed beyond your fondest hopes and your greatest expectations, you will never succeed beyond the purpose to which you are willing to surrender. Furthermore, your surrender will not be complete until you have formed the habit of doing the things failures do not like to do.

Chapter 4 – Ten Common Habits of Successful People

Do you remember how you used to be overly cautious when you were learning to drive? All your thoughts were about driving at the moment. You used to see a red light, and your mind would go: apply break! You couldn't even talk while driving. However, now that you have learned it, you don't think about it at all. You can drive from home to work while talking to your friend on call without a single conscious thought about driving. Driving has become an instinct to you; it has become a habit.

A habit is a valuable tool that, when used correctly, helps greatly in creating the momentum it takes to succeed. If you're not forming good habits deliberately, you will form bad habits unconsciously. ***A successful man is one who deliberately forms habits that help him achieve his idea of success.***

Your business is a reflection of the habits you've formed, and so is your current sales production. If you want to change your current sales production, then you need to change your habits. It is about cultivating your own work customs. Let's see how.

Any successful salesperson will tell you that it's easier to sell through referrals than it is to sell to cold prospects. If you have not deliberately formed the habit of asking for referrals on every sales call, then unconsciously, you have formed the habit of having to make your sales call to cold prospects. If you have not formed the habits of prospecting every day and asking for referrals on every call, then you will not outsell your competitors because they are doing what you're not doing. Successful sales habits don't end here; you must work a structured schedule to include time for appointments, traffic, prospecting daily, no matter what.

To be successful at your business, ***you need to become a walking, talking prospect selling machine.*** To become that, you need to change your habits. Machines don't go around slacking off, hanging out with friends late at night, spending money they don't have. They work as a habit. You must know too.

For that, you must really, really want it.

But before you decide to adopt these habits, let me tell you the most important habit you should form. It is the habit of keeping your promises to yourself.

I often wondered why did people slack off after receiving motivation from their friends and family or what made them forget their resolutions, especially when they were so pumped up when listening to motivational speeches or setting up goals. You must have done it too sometime. You would have left a seminar determined to things that would make you successful, only to find your decision and determination was not near as strong on that first Monday morning after the seminar.

The answer to that is simply the fact that people don't keep their promises to themselves.

Any decision you make is simply a promise to yourself. It isn't worth anything unless you have formed the habit of making and keeping the promises you promise to yourself, or unless right from the start, you link all those promises or goals with an emotional purpose that is strong enough to cause you to do the things that don't feel good.

Here's how you can keep that promise to yourself:

- link that promise to a strong emotional purpose
- measure your performance each day

Reviewing and measuring your promise each day causes you to decide each day. You not only measure the promise each day, but you keep it each day.

Now, if you miss a day, you must start all over again. But if you continue in the process of measuring and keeping your promises to yourself each day, you will finally wake up one morning a different person with a different feeling because your promises have been transformed into habits.

And, the reason you feel like a different person is because you have become the master of yourself and your likes and dislikes by discovering a purpose in life that is strong enough for you to override only doing the things that feel good. This new person is determined and ready to do what it takes.

Now, let's take a look at the ten promises you have to make and keep to yourself that will lead you to success. Remember, you have to do keep doing these until they are instilled in you and become a part of you.

1. SET GOALS

You cannot be successful if you haven't even decided to become successful. If you don't know where you're going, you will end up someplace you didn't plan to be.

Setting goals should be the number one priority for anyone seeking success. Define exactly what it is you want your end goal to be. Break it down to mini-goals. Make sure your reason for doing what you must do is strong, so when things go wrong, as they always tend to go at first, you have the strength and purpose of keeping going.

2. TAKE RESPONSIBILITY

Successful people take responsibility for their successes, failures, achievements, as well as mistakes.

Unlike the majority of the people, they don't play victim, neither do they let others take their credit. They spend their energies in the present and on planning for the future. You can do this too by asking questions like, "How can I make this work?" and "What can I learn from this?"

Remember: everyone suffers setbacks. When you suffer one, instead of wasting your time by playing the blame game, you have to use it as fuel to pump and push yourself towards a better future. You can also waste time when you celebrate mini goals too. Whatever the case may be, you have to decide what to do with your present and your future.

3. HAVE SELF-DISCIPLINE

Discipline is a strong trait of all successful people, and it is one that can easily be developed by being consistent.

Answer this: what do you when you're alone? Do you watch cat videos on YouTube, or do you do something that will be beneficial for your future? Again, the habit of setting goals comes in handy here. When you always have something clear to achieve, it is easier to work than to slack or be distracted.

4. WORK ON SELF DEVELOPMENT

You cannot really be successful if you have given up working on yourself.

Working on yourself doesn't mean that you hate yourself or are never satisfied; it just means that you never stop learning new things and growing into a better person.

5. READ, A LOT!

While it's true that not all readers are successful, all successful people are known to be readers.

These days, most people cannot even sit alone for two minutes without feeling bored and picking up their phones. On the other hand, successful people are those who are never bored as they're always working on something. When they have nothing to do, they use the time wisely to enhance their knowledge and their skills so that it can benefit their minds and their future.

If you are not a reader, try audiobooks. You can listen to them during a commute, or when you are working out, or if you ever feel like you're bored.

6. MANAGE TIME

It is no secret that time management is essential to success.

Unsuccessful people feel stressed and overwhelmed when they too much to do. Successful people are rarely fazed, however, as they prioritize the most important tasks first. They also plan in advance, days, months, or even years ahead, knowing clearly what needs to be done to complete their jobs and reach their goals. Without a sense of time management, you will not be able to develop even a single good habit, let alone be successful.

As Winston Churchill said:

"Success is not final; failure is not fatal. It's the courage to continue that counts."

7. TAKE RISKS

Let me put it simply: if you don't buy a lottery, you can't win the lottery.

Big rewards only follow big risks and big actions. A lot of people are scared of going big, for they fear failure. Successful people are also scared of failures, but they're more scared of regrets. They know that there will be times when they will need to take risks in order to get where they want or need to go.

You can either risk everything by going for the life you want or guarantee comfort by living a life you don't want.

8. DON'T GIVE IN

Nobody achieves all or any of their goals without failing at least once.

The difference between successful and unsuccessful people is in their approach when they're faced with failure. Unsuccessful people quit when faced with adversity; the successful, however, never quit. They keep going, knowing that their success story is being written in every moment and that it will be especially good with them making a comeback.

9. FIND A WAY TO WIN

If you want to win, you have to find a way to win. Period.

You have to have a whatever-it-takes mentality. It is the confidence in knowing that whatever happens, I will give my all and leave nothing on the table.

10. LOVE WHAT YOU DO

There is no easy path to success. But if you love doing what you do, the path does get easier.

I have been working in my custom clothing business for over three decades now. I never felt like I have a job. It's simply because I love what I do. If you are not doing what you love, you cannot be successful.

Money is not a success. You cannot trade your life working hours after hours for money and call yourself successful. If you have no other means of earning a decent living, do that. But make time for what you love. You live successfully only when you live working on the thing you love.

As they say:

"Do what you love, and you will never work a day in your life."

Success can mean different things to different people. For some, it could mean earning millions; for some, it could mean being recognized for their talent, while for yet others, it could mean living sustainably and happily with a small carbon footprint.

You get to define what being successful means to you too. But no matter what, these ten tips will help you achieve success. They apply to everyone and everyone's idea of success.

Chapter 5 – Networking

It's not work; it's ***NET****work.*

Why network, though?

I was a part of some business networking groups, but I was never very keen on seeing them every week. My excuse was that I did not have the time to have breakfast with a bunch of people at Denny's every week.

However, when we were hit by the real estate recession in 2008, I became desperate to try anything and everything. I started going to networking groups. I could see how they could be useful, but at the time, they didn't feel useful to me. I was not happy with the quality of the groups I was going to. I needed a higher-end group, but there wasn't any such group available.

I decided to start my own group. I made it a little different and a lot fancier. I held the group meetings at fancy places and charged $50 for it.

Long story short: it worked.

I had thought that if these businesspeople can afford a $50 breakfast, then they can afford my product too. I had thought, right. Soon, forty to fifty people were showing up weekly to my group.

Imagine having a virtual sales force of forty to fifty salespeople. I began receiving more and more leads every week and bounced back stronger than ever.

That whole ordeal taught me two things:

1. We should always take chances. It might just work.

If the chance I took by creating my own group hadn't worked, I would have taken some other chance. It taught me the "no excuses, just results" mentality.

2. The power of networking.

That is what I want to share with you in this chapter. I now call it the **ART of Networking**.

Networking is not a new idea. Everyone knows someone who can do something for someone else. Call it what you may: "old boy" networks, marital matchmakers, or people of influence; it is certainly not a new phenomenon. It is mirrored in every business in every culture, and in every country. However, when you look at networking as a skill for a businessperson, it becomes critical and takes new importance.

Today, seventy percent of businesses belong to one of the few business development groups or associations. Among the rest, thirty percent, twenty-five percent belong to two or more business development groups or associations.

Why is it that corporations are allotting financial resources to an unseen process that is difficult to qualify? Why is it that local and regional periodicals are providing a list of business events that include exchanging business cards and holding network meetings and events that tout networking opportunities? Why is it that databases are crammed with names of people that we just met and did conduct business with? Why is it that our calendars are packed with networking meetings?

The answer to all the above questions is the same: that networking is important, and its importance has been recognized.

The importance of networking has earned it an industry classification and has also pushed businesses to consider it as a necessary job skill and to create positions for it. The acceptance of networking as a business tool has led to the creation of several interesting opportunities.

It might sound harsh, but I just want to put it out there in honest words: if you're not part of the network, you will be crushed by it. It is the future, and your future will only be guaranteed if you network.

Let's looks at the ways in which networking has become important these days:

1. It has become a required job skill.
2. It is considered a learned skill.
3. Networking groups have become more valuable.
4. Networking is the impetus for strategic alliances and mergers.

5. Networking has become of the most important tools for business development.

If you or your company are not yet committed to the opportunities provided by networking, you better start now because good relationships pave the way for good business.

So, what can joining a business-networking group do for you and your business?

- It can increase your business.
- It helps you become better at public speaking.
- It gets you, loyal supporters.
- It gains you a reliable source of business and professionals to refer.
- It will get you the ***"feel-good factor"*** – that awesome feeling we get when we help someone succeed.

While aligning yourself and your company with other businesspeople and businesses is a sure way to encourage growth, don't expect it to happen overnight. Successful marketing takes more than merely knowing a lot of people. It takes a willingness to give information, ideas, resources, and leads without the expectation of a quick return. It also takes time. It takes time to build relationships, but their payoff is always worth it.

Remember, people like to do business with those they know and trust. It also applies to your networking group who can give you referrals.

People will only give you referrals when you have gained their respect. To earn their respect, you have to make sure that you make others around you feel that you are interested in helping them too. It requires taking the time to meet them, listening to them, and understanding what they need from you.

This will also help you become pro-active. It will inculcate in you the habit of checking up on or following up with things that you or your business might need later on. The pro-active approach will help you in all other aspects of your business too.

The quicker you and your networking partner understand each other's businesses and types of referrals needed, the quicker you will be able to make a strong bond with them.

Here are some questions you can ask your networking partner:

- What is your best client like?
- What are the benefits you and your firm offer your clients?

- Who makes the decision to use your product or service?
- What specifically should I say when I describe your company to one of my clients?

So, how do you get the most out of a business networking group?

GETTING THE MOST OUT OF BUSINESS NETWORKING GROUPS:

A network isn't merely a list of people's names or a collection of business cards. It is a group of people. To make the best of your networking group, you need to take the time to understand the business of each member in your network. If you have chosen the members wisely, this would be a lot of fun. You will get to meet some interesting people, with equally interesting businesses.

Now, the first way it can work for you is by educating them completely about what you do and whom you do it with. If they don't understand your business, they can't really give you useful referrals. Hence it is essential to make them understand what your business is about. Keep them updated, too, if there's anything new about your business or if you have altered the product or service in some way. Explain to them your business so well that they can refer to your business as well, if not better, as a hired salesperson would.

The second way in which the networking group can be of immense help to you is by not seeing it as something that would bring you clients alone. You should be able to turn to the members of your networking group for advice and ideas for management and leads, as well as vendor recommendations.

The networking group will be a success if all members learn from each other and each other's business and contribute to each other's growth both in terms of profit and performance.

CULTIVATING A NETWORK OF REFERRALS:

As a business person, when you meet someone new, you should have two goals:

1. Get to know as many people as possible
2. Get as many people as possible to know you

Networking is a two-way street. When you meet someone, you should want to ask them about their business and tell them about yours. Start with the basics – name, company, affiliation, position, nature of the business, etc. next, find out how you can both benefit each other. Make sure you ask them the following questions:

What does your company do?

What type of clients do you serve?

What makes the buying decision within a firm for each of your services or products?

What sets you apart from your competitors?

There's another, also a little more difficult, way to cultivate referrals is by looking for people who will be genuinely interested in helping others solve a problem. But where would you possibly find such people? The answer is simple: become one of these people. Don't think of yourself as a networker; instead, become a problem-solver for others. Like, attract like. When you become a problem-solver for others, you will be better able to judge and so find people who share this characteristic.

GET SMART ABOUT NETWORKING:

As your contact list grows, you should reevaluate people in your information loop on a regular interval. Prioritize those that are most useful to you. As you stay in touch with some more than others, those some will become your inner circle.

However, never burn bridges. You never know when someone might need your help, or you might need theirs. If you find someone as not useful to you at present, you should still check in with them time and again, as they may prove to be of importance to you down the road. In short, be nice to everyone. Niceness goes a long way. Also, things always change, and you never know when someone might show up.

In today's times of the prevalence of technology, it has become easier to stay in touch with people too. There are multiple social media apps nowadays that are dedicated solely to stay connected professionally. Stay active on such an app of your choice and interact with people. Post updates of your own business, or celebrate someone else's, send messages to people, or react to their posts. It will make you noticeable and will help people remember you too.

I would say as much; networking is the single most powerful tool for business development. As business owners, you must be aware that you have two full-time jobs. The first is to maintain the business and to keep existing clientele happy. The second job is to take measures to increase your market share and to make new clients.

Networking, when done correctly, provides you with opportunities to work smart and not hard. If you utilize your networking group members for the purpose of providing immediate quality solutions to problems that they're facing in their business, then that would mean you have topped the power of networking.

Chapter 6 – Lessons Learned from My Extremely Successful and Powerful Clients

I have had some amazing clients over my 30 plus year career. They were not absolutely amazing because they were successful, but they were amazing with how they did things, which led to their success.

When I decided to write this book, I reached out to some of them to learn more about them and their success. They agreed, and I have jotted down the questions I asked them, along with their answers in this chapter. I asked them all different questions, so there wouldn't be similar advice, and everyone can tell their unique approach towards different aspects of their business. I hope you all get to learn from them as much as I did.

Now, let's see what they had to say:

The first client who I interviewed is Brian Chase, a Managing Partner at the firm Bisnar Chase (www.bestattorney.com).

Qs: What was your purpose for being where you are now? Where did you come from, and where are you today?

Brian Chase: Let me talk about how I built my team first. For starters, we all know, or rather we all should know, "teamwork makes the dream work," so it's vitally important to build a great team. I cannot emphasize that enough.

One of my favorite business books is "Winning" by Jack Welsh. In that book, he has a great discussion on the 20/70/10 employee differentiation. He notes that "you embrace the top 20, deal with the middle 70, and you face into the bottom 10, and you do what's right for them and for you."

What he means by that is 20% of your employees are superstars or A players and that they are to be rewarded accordingly. You do not want to lose these people. You want to empower, motivate, and encourage them to grow and to want to stay with you.

The next 70% of your employees are not A-players or superstars yet, but they have the potential to become the A's. You want to send them to train, to motivate them with incentives, and give them a pathway to becoming A's.

The bottom 10% are people that you are ultimately going to have to let go of. Now, that may sound harsh, but I can tell you from personal experience when I have had to let a bottom 10%-er go, many have called me years later and thanked me. Yes, thanked me. You see, those bottom 10%-ers in your business are an A player or superstar in another business, and you are not doing them any favors keeping them on a team that you know they will ultimately fail on, and more importantly, prevent them from finding their true passion, a job where they can shine, be happy, and be a superstar.

I have had several of these people go on and start their own businesses and find their true passion. So, while it may sound mean-spirited to label someone in the bottom 10%, you are really doing right by them and yourself by letting them go.

Setting aside the 20/70/10 model, you need to have a great culture, and that does not just happen on its own. You must work at it. I have been fortunate in having my business labeled ***"The Best***

Places to Work in Orange County" *by the Orange County Business Journal for the past nine years in a row. That was no accident. We really strive and work at creating a great culture.*

For example, we have an annual staff meeting on the first workday of the year. We are very transparent, and we empower, motivate, and encourage the Team members. We go through last year's goals and see what teams within the company hit their financial goals. If they did, they are rewarded with, for example, a week's vacation in Hawaii with their spouse or significant other. If some teams did not hit their goal, but the over-all financial firm goal was reached, the entire firm and their spouses or significant others are sent on a nice week-long vacation, all paid for by the company. This not only motivates the team members but equally importantly, it gets their spouses or significant others bought into the company and its culture.

At this meeting, we set new goals for the year. We are very transparent with our finances, with the cases brought, and the source of those cases. We go through our mission statement and discuss good customer service, etc. At times, we bring in a motivational speaker to work with us too.

In addition to this, we have catered monthly birthday lunches where we celebrate the employee's or employee's birthday that month. We have occasional firm happy hours where we take an afternoon off and just go blow off steam and bond outside of the work environment. We do several other things like this too.

So, to build a great team, you need to identify your A's or superstars and develop those that are not yet A's to become A's. And one of the best ways to do that is to create a great culture for your team. I can't emphasize this enough; teamwork makes the dream work!

The second client of mine who I talked to for this book is Michael Papale. He is the CEO of Media Execution (www.mediaexecution.com).

This is how the conversation went with Michael:

Qs: What success principle would you teach people? Why would you teach that?

Michael Papale: Art, congratulations on your 2nd book. So very happy for you and proud of you! I'm honored that you would actually think of me and ask for my input.

Now, here's the answer to what you asked:

I have spent a lot of time thinking about this recently and over my career, and I came to this conclusion: yes, strategy, initiative, execution, and determination are critical. However, I personally believe that the number one success principle I would teach people would be ***ethics****. I always say, what's legal and what's ethical is, at times, not the same thing. For example, it was completely legal for numerous companies to apply for and receive PPP loans and SBA loans; however, it was not ethical for some of them.*

This is true with all leaders and the people they lead. It does not mean one is not savvy or shrewd; it means they make decisions that are honest and value the relationships internally as well as externally based on their actions and daily decisions, i.e., pay your partners on time. It is legal to pay net 60 or 90. How about net 15? Your partners will work harder for you, and your staff will respect you more. You will be successful, profitable, gain more market share, and lead in your space – which is the "why" of ethics!

The next client I talk to has been my client for over 20 years. His firm, Excellence RE, has over fifty-four offices and employees over 750 real estate agents.

He is Mike Oyoque, CEO of Excellence Real Estate (www.excellencere.com).

Qs. What do you think are your top three greatest strengths in sales?

Mike Oyoque: As I was walking on the path to success, my three strength as a human being were:

1. Dreaming Big – when you dream, it fuels your body.

2. Staying Persistent

3. Knowledge and Wisdom – that you and your product is the best that can be.

I wanted to ask a question to another successful client who became a close friend of mine, Rande Ferguson. Mr. Ferguson has been working both as a Fire Captain and a Fire Investigator for over 35 years.

Though he is not a businessman, Mr. Ferguson is highly successful at what he does. My conversation with him went like this:

Qs: What are the one or two things you absolutely love about your job?

Rande Ferguson: After thirty-five years, there are two specific items that I still love about being a firefighter regardless of rank or title.

The first is to have the opportunity to fulfill the needs of others in a time of absolute devastation in someone's life, not as in the "wants" of others, but as in a true need in a life or death situation. The second thing that I love about being a firefighter is that each shift is totally different from the previous shift; you never know what to expect. But what you do know is that with the teamwork of your crew, you "will" accomplish your mission, no matter what is thrown at you that particular day.

I also got to question my client Mr. Bob Bailey, who acts as both a Partner as well as a General Manager at Torre Nissan (www.torrenissan.com).

Qs. What do you think are your top three greatest strengths as a successful businessman?

Bob Bailey: Listening, caring, and trying to do the right thing even when it hurts.

The next client I talked to is Joe Vivanco from Lajoma Properties (www.lajomaproperties.com).

Qs. What do you think are your top three greatest strengths as a successful real estate agent?

Joe Vivanco: My three greatest strengths as a real estate agent are:

1. *I believe I'm a person with a professional approach.*
2. *I'm caring and understanding of my client's needs, and I treat them with respect and integrity.*

3. *I value their trust that they put in me to help them purchase their dream home.*

The majority of my clients become long term friends, and being their agent and being part of the journey with them, is the biggest reward for me.

Thank you for thinking of me to help you with your book.

The next client that I learned from is Ron Feder. Mr. Feder is the Managing Director for KW Commercial Calabasas (www.rjfeder.com). I asked him the same question as I did Mr. Michael Papale.

Qs: What success principle would you teach people?

Ron Feder: Art, Good morning! Thank you for thinking of me, buddy! I truly admire the way you run your business.

Now, to answer the question,

The number one success principle I deploy is under-promise and over-perform. Too often, salespeople tell you they will get back to you tomorrow and don't. I tell someone that I will get back to them by 5 pm tomorrow and then call them at 4 pm. It truly builds credibility.Another principle that I have is to not lie. If someone asks a question that I do not know, I tell them that I do not know but that I will find out and get back to them. The more times you interact with your clients, the better.

I also focus on the client first. If I do my job well, I will definitely earn a fee. Too many salespeople focus on the dollar and so neglect the client's needs and don't do their job well.

Again, I appreciate you thinking of me. If you need anything else, please do not hesitate.

Stay healthy!

The last client of mine that I approached for this book and got to learn from is Rod Gordy. Rod is the Senior Vice President for Fidelity National Title Company. Fidelity has been winning the title of ***#1 Title Company for 21 consecutive years now.***

Qs: In your opinion, what are the three habits that can improve your life?

Rod Gordy: Art Lewin Bespoke, thank you for being my tailor, friend, and influencer for over 30 years!

At the age of 62 and still winning, I wear your custom shirts, bespoke suits, and ties five days a week! I'm often told by people that I am the sharpest dressed executive in the Title Insurance industry. The credit for these compliments goes to you. I know you are also the Bespoke Tailor to many of the other sales executives as well as many of my clients. You are a legend in Los Angeles. Thank you for the excellent service!

I apologize that my thoughts on your question "what are the three habits that can improve your life?" for your new book is coming in two weeks late. But here they are, and they are more than three thoughts.

From the age of seventeen to now sixty-two years, these thoughts have been the mantra that I have been loyal to.

1. Surround yourself with people you respect and want to become in life and business, learn from them, and mirror them.

2. Find out your why when setting your goals each year. It will help you find how to achieve them.

3. Consistently take baby steps to your goals and never give up.

4. Passion and persistence overcome fear and uncertainty.

5. My mantra to my sales force, and my boys is ***"Attitude is Everything!"***

6. Done is better than perfect – go for it!

7. Keep your family first.

Good luck, Art. I am sure your book will be another best seller!

I want to thank all my clients for being so kind, generous, and honest with their answers. I really hope that you, my readers, can apply their mantras to your life and business practice and benefit from it.

Chapter 7 – Twelve Ways to Get More Business

Who doesn't want more business from clients and prospects? I mean, if you're reading this book, then there's a hundred percent chance that you want to grow your business.

Now, how do you grow a business? The answer to that is simple: by growing your clientele. And below are my 12 ways to help you achieve exactly that!

GAME PLAN 1 – DO MULTIPLE FOLLOW-UPS

The first way to increase your clientele is to focus on those leads who can become your clientele but haven't become it yet. I always tell salespersons to work on their unconverted leads until they buy, die, or shoo you away.

Now when I say focus on them, I mean that you should make them your number one priority. Keep working on those numbers by doing multiple follow-ups. Most businesses give up far too easily; don't do it like most businesses.

When someone emails you or makes a call to you to ask about what you have to offer, you get a record of that person. About 90% of the businesses get approached by a client this way, and they usually reply to the email or call this person back. They might send some brochures or some additional information in the email too. That would be it. Once or twice is the number of times they will follow-up with that customer. I've personally have pursued a prospect for over 5, 10, 20 plus years.

It has been proven through research, again and again, that it takes about seven points of contacts to convert a lead into a customer, to convert a potential customer into a buying customer.

This information is super interesting to me as a salesperson, and I'm sure it would be of interest to you too, along with being useful.

Now, the form of contact can vary depending on the business. However, the theory stands true.

On average, your customer will need an email, then another email, and then maybe a phone call, then another email after that, then maybe something else in the email, then maybe an in-person meetup if it's appropriate, and then another email or two. Only then will they become a customer.

It may sound like a long process, but you absolutely have to and need to make multiple follow-ups. If someone is coming within a mile of your business, you have to make sure that your follow-ups bring them all the way to your business's outlet. To make sure this happens, you have to have a system in place that uses emails, phone calls, or other marketing and communication forms to bring the client to your business's doorstep.

GAME PLAN 2 – REFERRALS

The second way to get more clients is through your existing clients. Before you spend money on marketing and advertising, encourage your existing customers to get you new customers through referrals.

There is nothing new about people referring businesses to each other. Every business gets referrals. Some businesses actually exist on them. However, common as though it may be, referrals are always accidentals. When you look at them from the perspective of business owners, they always happen by accidents as the business owner does nothing to get them, except providing a good product or service to their customer. Business owners, in this case, are not proactively looking for referrals. In fact, they're just doing their job.

But I want you to be proactive about this. I want you to understand the importance of having a system in place – a system that would develop a referral culture. A referral culture requires your customers to understand that referrals are a core part of how you grow and that they, as one half of that customer-business relationship, almost have an obligation to give referrals.

I know it sounds too strong, but it is entirely possible that too effectively. How, you ask? You do it by building it into a system that would require you to have a dialogue with the customer when they first become your customer. you can say, ***"I built my business primarily through word-of-mouth recommendations from people like yourself. If I do a great job for you, would you be willing to recommend me to your friends, family, and colleagues?"***

Now, do you think someone would say no to that?

Of course not!

It works simply because you're putting the idea in people's heads that if they're happy with your product or service, they will get you referrals. You made a deal with them, and when you deliver your part of it well, they will definitely deliver your part too.

Imagine, if every individual that became a customer brought one more customer with them, and then this second person brought another, third, customer to you, then you'd never have to spend any money on advertising or marketing.

That is the sheer power of referrals! Therefore, always ask for them.

GAME PLAN 3 – IMPROVE SALES SKILLS

One of the things that can prove extremely beneficial for you is understanding the art and science of getting customers. Now I can rattle all about it in specific ways, for example, *"do this on the second page of your website."* But if you really want to become a pro at getting customers, you must be able to practice the art of it, which is the slightly intangible element of sales.

The ability to sell effectively is as important to the ability to get customers as anything, and it will always be this important. If you have a team, this applies to your team too.

I'm noting this down here because most business owners are not going into the business to sell. They don't go into their business thinking, ***"I'd like to leave this lousy job I'm in and spend all day selling things to people."*** They don't think of owning their own business as a job where they have to sell something day and night. It's because most don't particularly like the idea of selling. Most go into business either because they want to get out of the job they're in or because they are motivated to offer a particular service or product to the world. Now, both of these are great reasons;

however, they are not enough – not enough to be successful at least. Success in business just boils down to two things: sales and marketing.

It doesn't matter if you're looking to grow an already established company or starting a small business from your garage; you'll still be called an entrepreneur. And as an entrepreneur, you have to know how to sell. This is required not only for you to sell your product or service yourself but also to know if the key people in your team are doing it right or not.

If at this point you have realized that you're not as great at selling as you should be, then don't worry. It is a skill that anyone can learn and improve. There are various ways to improve it too, e.g., taking courses, reading books, attending seminars, or even observing good salespersons making sales. It doesn't matter what way you pick to improve your skills; my core message here to you is that you need to understand the fundamental importance of sales as part of the customer attraction and acquisition strategy for your business.

George Foreman, the two-time world heavyweight champion, Olympic gold medalist, and entrepreneur, said that if he could teach his children one thing in life, it would be the art of selling. If you can sell, you will never lose your home or be short of money because good salespeople are always in demand.

I'm sure that as a business owner, you already know this. Wouldn't you love some great salespeople to walk in the door tomorrow? Yes, right?

So, you are aware that the ability to sell is one of life's most important skills.

GAME PLAN 4 – OVERCOME OBJECTIONS

This is another aspect that most business owners tend to ignore, yet it is another incredibly important one. Most business owners focus on the thought that looks something like, ***"I want more customers. So, where should I place the advert for maximum exposure?"*** I wouldn't say that's not important. It is, but once you have grabbed their attention, you also need to overcome any objections they might have to the sale.

Let's turn the tables and think of it this way:

What is it that's stopping you from getting more customers?

You are already following up on leads. You also know that every business has its own unique conversion rate, which is the number of people contacting a business and becoming its customers.

The leads will be the number of people who visit your business's website, walk into your business, or make a phone call to enquire about your business, but this number will never be converted to customers. The conversion rate from your leads to customers would be anything between 1-60, depending on who you are, where you are, what is it that you're doing. For most businesses, it is usually under 50%.

You have to understand that once you have paid for marketing and advertising to bring people close to becoming your customers, then you have already paid the cost for it, so if you work on increasing the conversion rate, you're just increasing the efficiency of both your time and money.

Tell me something, why would anyone go to the trouble of visiting your business's website or fill in a form or pick up the phone to call you but then not buy? The lead is already interested in what you're selling. If it is of good value and meets their need, why wouldn't the conversion rate be a hundred percent?

The answer to the above questions is customer objections. The thing that stops the sale is rarely the business's lack of customer's need or want. It is the objection in the customer's head.

Some of the big objections are time and money. The customer thinks, ***"it's too expensive,"*** or ***"I don't have the time to invest in this."***

The objections to your business will be specific to your business. If you pay attention to these leads and to your customers, the objections that are specific to your business will become clear to you. When they begin becoming clear to you, list them down, and then work out smart answers to these objections. You will soon be able to answer them correctly and increase the percentage of your leads to customers' conversion rate.

While most business owners are unaware of the objections altogether, some come up with excuses that sound something like, ***"I haven't got time for this. I'm busy."*** To these business owners, I say: If you're a business owner yet are reluctant to spend at least 3 out of the 365 days of a year immersed in cutting-edge internet marketing because you believe you're too busy, then you have a problem!

GAME PLAN 5 – ASK FOR THE SALE

This one is ridiculously obvious but is also super important.

Ask for the sale. It's as simple as that. It's a tragedy how many salespeople and business owners do everything right when communicating with a potential customer – presenting what they have, answering questions, even overcoming objections – yet when it comes to the key moment to say, ***"should we confirm the order then?"*** or ***"how would you like to pay?"*** they don't say it. I don't understand why they don't do it. It might have to do with some psychological hang-ups. But you get the idea.

Ask for the sale. Make sure your team asks for the sale too.

There are usually a number of people involved in a business. If you think any of them is not a salesperson, then think again. In their own way, from your receptionist to your manager, all are salespeople. And anybody who is involved in sales should be awarded and compensated for the way they're linked to the sale.

Fifteen years ago, I went into companies to talk about influence and sales skills to their sales teams. I was shocked to find out how many sales teams were on a flat salary and did not receive a commission. Instead, the sales manager would tell them, *"we will have doughnuts at the team meeting on Friday."* I don't know anyone who would make an extra call on a cold, wet Wednesday afternoon for a doughnut. So, I don't know why anyone would compensate anyone for donuts. It is not adequate or even appropriate.

GAME PLAN 6 – SEND MORE EMAILS

One year, I sent out over 200,000 emails.

Why did I do that? Let's talk about it.

There's a simple rule for email marketing: send out more emails, get more customers.

You should be sending out at least one email, if not more, to each of your customers every month. Ideally, you should have a relationship with them where you can send them more than one email every month since not every email is a sales marketing email. Some of the emails are to add value by giving useful information.

According to a 2020 study, the number of email users by 2021 will be more than 3.8 billion, which is over a hundred million more than it was only last year. It tells us that the use of email is increasing rapidly year-on-year and that it is also becoming many people's preferred way of communication. This popularity in the use of emails is extremely beneficial to businesses as it allows them to tap into customers worldwide without any additional cost. More importantly, when people subscribe to businesses with their emails, it means that they already want to hear from that business. There can't be a better opportunity for businesses! Capitalize on that. Send more emails.

GAME PLAN 7 – USE DIRECT MAIL

Direct mail has been an incredible way of getting customers into any business for over a hundred years now.

However, these days it is not used by small businesses as much as it should be. People are more enthusiastic about using the internet, and generally, I'm well-known for preaching the use of digital marketing and advertising too. But I don't understand why new businesses ignore direct mail when it is still a perfectly valid source of gaining new customers.

There is a huge challenge when it comes to gaining new customers. You have to get someone who doesn't know you and has never spent money with you to give you money. While the internet has made it considerably easier to achieve, there is still a big proportion of the population that value physical things they can literally hold in their hands before they give their money.

If you take some time to look at what comes through your home or office letterbox, you will find a lot of business mail in there. Now let me tell you, direct mail is not cheap. But so many businesses still send it because it still really works.

The beauty of direct mail lies in it being personal to every customer. how can you not open a mail with your name on it? It is the most effective way for businesses to have a conversation with customers in their kitchen or as they sit in their garden.

While here, I've brought this up to get more clients, but it can always be used for existing clients. It is, in fact, much easier to get your existing customers to spend money with you through any form of marketing, including direct mail. So you should definitely want to do it with existing customers. But I hope you try it out to get new customers too.

GAME PLAN 8 – TESTIMONIALS

I hope that by now, you're able to see the many ways to get new customers. The strategy of putting up testimonials can be applied to direct mail, but it essentially works with many different marketing types, like emails. You can even put them on the website.

So, why should you use testimonials? Well, because they're a great way of getting more customers. There is a proportion, probably around 30-40 percent, for whom social proof is a key element of their buying decision. It is when they receive social proof that they think, ***"everybody else is doing this. I should try it too!"*** If you need proof of the social proof, then look no further than the iPhone.

Everybody has an iPhone. Everybody else is going to the Apple Store to get one. Social proof is important, and for a good chunk of the population, it is important to the extent that they won't do business with you if there isn't some social proof. Case studies and real-life stories from people who have experienced and benefitted from using their product or service cannot fail to increase your sales.

If you meet customers face-to-face, you will want to pull out a book of testimonials. But the best time to pull them out is when a customer comes up with the objections I mentioned earlier. If the customer says, *"Your product is a bit expensive,"* you can reply by saying, *"Can I show you something? Here are some people who raised the price issue, and here's what happened when they went ahead and did business with us. Here are their stories."*

So, testimonials can be of immense help to you. Use them.

GAME PLAN 9 – DIRECT SALES

This is one of the biggies.

It refers to having a salesperson or a sales team go out into the real world and get sales. I did this for over twenty years, and I still do it.

It is one of the obvious strategies, but it can get ignored, especially since everyone is drawn towards the internet and the things happening on the internet. But there are so many different kinds of businesses that can still benefit from having people go out into the field and making sales for them.

One of the things that astound me while watching documentaries on TV is where they find a troubleshooter to fix a small business, but never actually show or mention them visiting people all day every day, knocking on doors, selling stuff. It's scary, yes. But that's the way to be, and you should try it out too. I highly encourage you to add a direct sales element to your business if you don't already have one.

GAME PLAN 10 – CALL TO ACTION

Each and every form of advertising and marketing that you put out, be it an ad, a message, or an email, should include a proper call to action or CTA. CTA is important because it tells people what to do.

I mentioned earlier how salespeople or business owners often don't ask for the sale; the same is true for many marketing pieces and ads. They can be well-made, but they can fail to be compelling by not letting people know what to do next. The key to getting more customers, especially new customers, is to tell them precisely what to do. Tell them, ***"go to the website ..."*** or ***"pick up your phone now and dial ..."***

It may sound obvious. It may even sound like a bit too much, but it's not. People are usually always busy, and more often than not, they need leading. So, it's your duty to tell them what to do to approach your business.

GAME PLAN 11 - SELL BENEFITS, NOT FEATURES

Always talk about the benefits the customer can get from your product or service, and never mention the features that you are offering. A great number of salespeople still make this fundamental marketing mistake and make it often.

Now, if you want to buy a home stereo system and the salesperson begins telling you about how many decibel levels are coming out of the woofer or how the stereo system took 19 hours to be made in Taiwan, then unless you're a complete stereo system geek, you wouldn't care less about all the things the salesperson is telling you.

Most people would lose interest in listening to such a sales pitch because the salesperson would only be listing product features to them and wouldn't be informing how it can benefit the customer.

If they start listing the benefits, however, then they would tell you how the stereo system will look beautiful in your home, how it will provide you with great quality sound, and how when you play music on it, it will make you feel like you're attending a concert while at your own home.

To make a great sales pitch, you need to know what is important to your customer. some people buy an 85" flat screen TV to impress their neighbors. If that's what your customer needs, then you need to hammer home on that. If you're selling hammers, you won't sell the hammer or the hole in the wall, you will sell the ability to put an amazing photograph or painting on the wall and the joy the person will feel every time they look at it.

Apply this. Learn to apply this. Look at all your marketing, particularly the parts that get the most attention, like your business's website's homepage. Start telling your customers the benefits of your product or service within the first couple of sentences.

GAME PLAN 12 – BE AN AUTHORITY; WRITE A BOOK

A great way to become an authority in the field of your business is by writing a book.

I give this advice to everyone. Most of the time, people react with, *"I work in a very mundane industry. What would I write about?"* I never tell people to write a best-seller, which is fine if they want to do that, but I just tell people to write a book. The truth is that most non-fiction books have a pretty low readership level, so when I talk about writing a book, I talk about writing a book purely to give you a position of authority.

Write a book or get a ghostwriter to write a book with you on the areas in your business that you are an expert on. These areas could be technical or even mass-market; it doesn't matter; it's your choice. Write what you know the most about.

In my years of dealing with people, I have learned that most people have specific knowledge that can prove to be useful to other people. Put that specific knowledge that you have in a book.

Even if you self-publish and only print a thousand copies, the purpose is not to have your books fill shelves upon shelves in bookstores; it is for your customers to see that you're an author of a book. It gives you instant credibility. Secondly, you can use that book as a marketing tool. You will often find smart marketers giving away books as a free gift on their websites or in their ads.

Writing a book has wonderful impacts. It helps you gain credibility and gives you authority, and it's also a great early sale or leads generational tool. Give it some thought. You're here because you want more customers. If you do it, you will get more customers.

I believe everybody can write a book. You may have a book idea in your mind already that somebody else will publish. Also, just so you know, you can be fairly sure that about four to six thousand people will buy your non-fiction book, and you will probably get someone to publish it too. If not, publish it yourself. It is not a significantly huge investment.

Chapter 8 – My Thoughts

I'd like to begin the end of this book with the following quote from entrepreneur Jim Rohn. He said,

"You're the average of the five people you spend the most time with."

I think of this quote often, and the more I think of it, the more I find it to be true.

We should all try our best to surround ourselves with people who do interesting things, who think interesting thoughts, who challenge us to be better versions of ourselves, and who come from diverse backgrounds. The company of such people combined with some much needed "me time," provides us with the perfect breeding ground to generate great ideas.

Now, in whichever field you seek success, never get hung up on what your competitors are doing. It's one thing to be aware of the latest trends in the industry you work in, and a very different thing to let others' work hinder your creative process.

YEAR-ROUND SUCCESS

Let me share a well-thought-out, as well as tried and tested method to seek success all year round.

- Make yourself 52 promises that would push you towards achieving success – one for every week of the year
- Set 12 goals for yourself that would act as steps towards your success – one for every month of the year

Now, ask/tell yourself the following five points to motivate yourself every day:

1. What's the daily success schedule like?
2. Learn to Delegate more.
3. Where are you now?
4. Where do you want to go from here?
5. What do you want?

GIVING SPEECH – 101

Here are my tips for giving speeches:

Learn the mechanics of giving a speech first. It includes the following:

- opening
- body
- pace
- vocal variety
- conclusion
- pause

- state movement enthusiasm
- body movement

You should also be aware of the life force elements of a speech. These are:

- conviction
- passion
- sincerity
- humility

another advice I'd give you for giving speeches would be the cliched, ***"be yourself and just talk to the audience."*** I'm a fan of this advice because many people, when trying for *public speaking*, instead begin *public reading.*

While not everyone is born as a public speaker, "talking" is something that everyone does. It is common as well as the natural state of communication. And most people, when someone is talking to them, pay them their attention anyway.

The last advice I'd add for giving great speeches is: tell a story. A story captures people's attention a lot more than a set of facts and information. Therefore, always tell a story to make a point. Observe good storytellers learn the how-to of storytelling.

I believe anyone can be successful. Why? Because I was an anyone, in fact, no one, at a time. I started from the bottom. Here's why I say:

wake up, kick-ass, and repeat!

DEALING WITH FAILURE

This is another one of my go-to pieces of advice for every entrepreneur I come across: fall in love with the F word (F word being a failure).

Whenever you're faced with failure, ask yourself: what is my driving force? You need to remember your reason of why you started in the first place, the most at that time.

John Wooden said,

"Failure is a must in success. Success is never final; failure is never fatal."

THE RARITY OF SUCCESS

Do you know that there's a 92% chance of success if you go for brain surgery? Do you also know that there's only a 2.4% chance of success if you start a new business? Success in business is a rarity. However, there are some tips and tricks that can help you make this rarity into your reality.

It begins with sales, and while beginning a sale, you should be mindful of two things: to be different from other salespeople and to be emotional, since every decision is an emotional decision for consumers. Yes, it is emotions that make people buy overpriced tickets to Disneyland and wait up to six hours in line. ***People's emotions are what run businesses.***

NOTES ON SALES

Selling is never about pricing; it is always about emotions, senses, and feelings. People buy what they find value in. to sell them your product, you must create value in the product. When listening to your sales pitch, customers are not engaged in a battle of logic. They need to be motivated to buy the product by showing them its value.

Let's look at some of the fundamentals of sales:

1. Creating Trust – this includes establishing enough agreement to counter sales resistance with sales acceptance.
2. Credibility – refers to image and reputation
3. Negative Post – induce a fear of missing out, push the fear of loss, and create urgency

Remember, you cannot sell what you do not own!

Bonus Tip: Refer your potential customers to some written information on your product.

ESTABLISHING TRUST

Trust is established on the following eight pillars:

1. clarity
2. compassion
3. character
4. competence
5. commitment
6. connection
7. contribution
8. consistency

PURPOSE OF LIFE

Life should always be purpose-driven. If someone doesn't have a purpose in their life, their life loses all meaning. With purpose, life is a gift. Without purpose, life is a burden.

If you have a purpose, yet you still feel lazy, then you should either change the tools you're working with, change the people you're surrounded by, or change the purpose itself. A strong enough purpose doesn't let anyone lie on the couch all day.

COMMITMENTS TO SELF

Make the following commitments to yourself and follow-through:

- Be an inspiration
- Obey all rules
- Value your time
- Be yourself – don't let anyone beat you to it
- Live your life
- Don't wish for things; work for things – you don't always get what you wish for, but you always get what you work for

- Be seen, be heard, be noticed
- Dress in style – style gets noticed; substance takes it from there

---

In the end, remember this:

"Success is not a destination; it's a journey.

ABOUT THE AUTHOR

ART LEWIN
Bespoke
Since 1989

#1 INDEPENDENT CUSTOM CLOTHIER IN THE COUNTRY BY VOLUME

Representing Some of the Most Influential Clients in the World

- **AMERICA'S PREMIER BESPOKE CLOTHIER**
  AMERICAN EXPRESS
- **THE GURU OF CUSTOM CLOTHING**
  FOX 11, MY FOX LA
- **VOTED #1 CUSTOM CLOTHIER IN LOS ANGELES**
  LA DOWNTOWN NEWS
- **LOS ANGELES BEST CUSTOM TAILORS**
  LOS ANGELES TIMES

Art Lewin
Art Lewin Bespoke
800-994-7848
art@artlewin.com.com
www.ArtLewinBespoke.com

BESPOKE SUITS I CUSTOM SHIRT MAKERS I EXPERT TAILORING I FOR MEN AND WOMEN

Art Lewin is a son, a father, a husband, and a friend. He is also an entrepreneur and a real estate investor, as well as the owner and creative director of Executive Clothiers, one of the United States' premier bespoke clothing companies and the leading clothier to California's corporate stars as well as some Hollywood celebrities. Mr. Lewin is also one of the leading experts on direct marketing and corporate image consulting.

Mr. Lewin sat on the executive committee and used to chair the membership committee at the City Club Los Angeles. He is also the founder of Professional Business Network (PBN), a group with more than ten thousand online members. Founder of Healthy Choice Labs and a real estate investor. Mr. Lewin and his work have been featured by a number of publications and broadcasters, some of which are the Los Angeles Times, CNN TV, the Wall Street Journal, GQ, Beverly Hills Lifestyle Magazine, Hispanic Businesses, Fox 11 News, Entrepreneur, Esquire, Los Angeles Business Journal, Forbes, CSQ, American Express, Inc. Magazine, ClubCorp, the

Hollywood Reporter, Confidential, just to name a few.

Mr. Lewin resides both in Indian Wells and in Los Angeles. In his spare time, he enjoys fine dining, working out, reading, traveling, and hanging out with his family and friends. He can be reached through email at art@artlewin.com. Mr. Lewin is also available on Facebook, Instagram, Twitter, YouTube, and LinkedIn.

ABOUT ART LEWIN BESPOKE

Art Lewin Bespoke is a distinguished provider of bespoke tailoring services based in Los Angeles, renowned for crafting custom-made suits, shirts, and formal wear for both men and women.

With a rich history dating back to 1989, Art Lewin Bespoke has established itself as the go-to tailor for Southern California's business elite and celebrities, offering unparalleled customization options.

Art Lewin Bespoke prides itself on a personalized approach, ensuring each garment is meticulously tailored to fit the precise measurements and preferences of its clients. Their materials are sourced from the world's finest mills in Italy, England, Scotland, and France, allowing a range of over 4,000 distinctive cloths.

Art Lewin's expert tailors work in-house to create pieces that embody individuality and elegance, underpinning their commitment to 100% satisfaction guaranteed.

Beyond its bespoke suiting, the company is also known for its expert alterations, invisible reweaving, and a selection of private label suits, demonstrating a comprehensive dedication to meeting every client's sartorial needs.

But that's us describing us; read below how some major publications have described us:

The Guru of Custom Clothing

MyFoxLA

America's Premier Custom Clothier.

American Express

Best Custom Tailors in Los Angeles.

Fox News 11

Voted #1 Custom Clothier in Los Angeles.

LA Downtown News

California's Businessman of the Year.

Wall Street Journal

Top 50 fastest minority-owned businesses in LA.

Los Angeles Business Journal

Nominated as Businessman of the Year.

California Chamber of Commerce

Top 100 National Hispanic Entrepreneurs.

Hispanic Magazine

One of the Best Dressed Men in America.

Esquire

Listed on the national prestigious Inc. 500/5000 list.

INC Magazine

www.ingramcontent.com/pod-product-compliance
Lightning Source LLC
LaVergne TN
LVHW022057200926
848481LV00003B/947